# Recipes to Remember

## Breakfast

## Lunch

## Dinner

*Campbell's*

FAMILY-CENTERED MEALTIMES

# Breakfast

Reclaim
breakfast
time as
family time,
with these
great-tasting
(but fast and
easy) meals

## ITALIAN FRITTATA

**PREP TIME:** 15 MINUTES
**COOK TIME:** 15 MINUTES

2 **tablespoons butter** *or* **margarine**

½ **cup chopped onion**

8 **eggs**

1 **cup shredded fontina cheese**

½ **cup seeded, chopped tomato**

2 **tablespoons chopped fresh parsley**

⅛ **teaspoon pepper**

2 **tablespoons grated Parmesan cheese**

1 **cup Prego® Traditional Pasta Sauce**

**Sliced cherry tomatoes, fresh basil leaves (optional)**

**PREHEAT** broiler.

**HEAT** butter in 10-inch ovenproof skillet. Add onion and cook until tender.

**BEAT** eggs. Stir in fontina cheese, tomato, parsley and pepper. Add to skillet. Reduce heat to low. Cook 6 minutes or until eggs are set 1 inch from edge. Do not stir. Sprinkle with Parmesan.

**BROIL** 6 inches from heat 5 minutes or until golden brown.

**HEAT** pasta sauce in saucepan until hot. Cut into wedges. Serve with pasta sauce. Garnish with tomatoes and basil leaves if desired. Serves 4.

## CLASSIC CAMPBELLED EGGS

**PREP/COOK TIME:** 15 MINUTES

1 **can (10¾ ounces) Campbell's® Cream of Chicken or 98% Fat Free Cream of Chicken Soup**

8 **eggs**

   **Dash pepper**

2 **tablespoons butter or margarine**

   **Chopped fresh parsley or chives**

**STIR** soup until smooth. Beat in eggs and pepper.

**HEAT** butter in skillet. Add egg mixture. Cook until set but still very moist, stirring lightly. Sprinkle with parsley. Serves 4.

**VARIATION** *For a change of pace, sprinkle with shredded Cheddar cheese just before serving.*

## Kitchen Notes

My mother-in-law is a great cook. She often shares her cooking secrets with me. One for which I am eternally grateful is her method for chopping fresh parsley. When I tried to chop parsley on a cutting board, it flew everywhere. She told me to put the parsley into a small plastic juice glass, then snip it with kitchen shears. It works like a charm!

—*Jane*

## FRENCH TOAST CASSEROLE

**PREP TIME:** 15 MINUTES    **CHILL TIME:** 1 HOUR
**COOK TIME:** 50 MINUTES

1 loaf (16 ounces) Pepperidge Farm® Cinnamon Swirl Bread, cut into cubes (about 8 cups)

6 eggs, beaten

3 cups milk

2 teaspoons vanilla extract

Confectioners' sugar

**PLACE** bread cubes in greased 3-quart shallow baking dish. Mix eggs, milk and vanilla. Pour over bread. Cover and refrigerate 1 hour or overnight. **Uncover**.

**BAKE** at 350°F for 50 minutes or until golden. Sprinkle with confectioners' sugar. Serve with pancake syrup, if desired. Serves 8.

## HAM & CHEESE HASH BROWNS

**PREP/COOK TIME:** 25 MINUTES

- 1 tablespoon butter *or* margarine
- ½ cup chopped cooked ham
- 1 medium onion, sliced
- ¼ cup diced green *or* sweet red pepper
- 1 can (10¾ ounces) Campbell's® Cheddar Cheese Soup
- ½ cup milk
- 1 teaspoon prepared mustard
- 4 cups frozen diced potatoes (hash browns)

**HEAT** butter in skillet. Add ham, onion and pepper and cook until vegetables are tender-crisp.

**ADD** soup, milk, mustard and potatoes. Heat to a boil. Cover and cook over low heat 10 minutes or until potatoes are tender. Serves 6.

**VARIATION** *For a creative twist, use frozen shredded potatoes and garnish with chopped green onions.*

Kitchen Notes

My mother almost never cried when she peeled, sliced, or chopped onions. Her secret? She always poured a few drops of white distilled vinegar on the knife and cutting board before she started. She claimed it neutralized the strong fumes that make people cry.

—*Cindy*

## FESTIVE BREAKFAST CASSEROLE

**PREP TIME:** 15 MINUTES    **CHILL TIME:** 2 HOURS
**COOK TIME:** 45 MINUTES

8 ounces bulk pork sausage

6 cups Pepperidge Farm® Distinctive Original White Bread, cut in cubes

1½ cups shredded Cheddar cheese

1 cup Pace® Picante Sauce *or* Chunky Salsa

4 eggs

¾ cup milk

**COOK** sausage until browned. Pour off fat.

**ARRANGE** sausage in 2-quart shallow baking dish. Top with bread cubes and cheese. Mix picante sauce, eggs and milk and pour over all. Cover and refrigerate 2 hours or overnight. **Uncover**.

**BAKE** at 350°F for 45 minutes or until done. Serves 6.

## BREAKFAST TACOS

**PREP/COOK TIME:** 20 MINUTES

1 tablespoon butter *or* margarine

1 cup diced, cooked potato

4 eggs, beaten

4 slices bacon, cooked, drained and crumbled

4 flour tortillas (8-inch)

¾ cup shredded Cheddar cheese

½ cup Pace® Picante Sauce

**HEAT** butter in skillet. Add potato and cook until lightly browned. Add eggs and bacon and cook until eggs are set but still moist, stirring often.

**WARM** tortillas according to package directions. Spoon **about ½ cup** potato mixture down center of each tortilla. Top with cheese and picante sauce. Fold tortilla around filling. Makes 4 tacos.

**VARIATION** *For another tasty breakfast sandwich, use crumbled cooked pork sausage instead of bacon.*

# Lunch

**Remember how great it was,** racing home to see what Mom was making for lunch? There's nothing like a homemade lunch to remind your family you're thinking of them.

Who needs fast food? These lunches feed your family homemade, wholesome goodness in short order!

## SOUPERBURGER SANDWICHES

**PREP/COOK TIME:** 15 MINUTES

1 pound ground beef

1 medium onion, chopped

1 can (10¾ ounces) Campbell's® Tomato Soup

1 tablespoon prepared mustard

⅛ teaspoon pepper

6 hamburger rolls

COOK beef and onion in skillet until browned. Pour off fat.

ADD soup, mustard and pepper and heat through. Serve in rolls. Makes 6 sandwiches.

**VARIATION** *For a Southwestern treat, wrap up Souperburger filling in warmed flour tortillas.*

**Campbell's®**

# The Possibilities of Tomato Soup

We all know that **Campbell's® Tomato Soup** has been a family
favorite for years. Take everyday ingredients, and
create your own favorite flavor
combination . . . the possibilities are endless!

■

**Cheese:** Shredded cheese of any
variety makes a simple stir-in that
adds great flavor.

**Croutons:** Wake up your
lunch with a little bit of
crunch!

**Pizza Soup:** Stir in shredded
mozzarella cheese, pepperoni
slices, and oregano for a taste
of your take-out favorite
any time!

**Taco Soup:** Stir in salsa and sour
cream, then top with shredded
cheese and crumbled tortilla chips
for a taste of the Southwest.

## 2-BEAN CHILI

**PREP/COOK TIME:** 25 MINUTES

1 **pound ground beef**

1 **large green pepper, chopped**

1 **large onion, chopped**

2 **tablespoons chili powder**

¼ **teaspoon pepper**

3 **cups Campbell's® Tomato Juice**

1 **can (about 15 ounces)** *each* **kidney beans** *and* **great Northern beans, rinsed and drained**

**Sour cream, sliced green onions, shredded Cheddar cheese, chopped tomato**

**COOK** beef, green pepper, onion, chili powder and pepper in skillet until browned. Pour off fat.

**ADD** tomato juice and beans and heat through. Top with sour cream, green onions, cheese and tomato. Serves 6.

**TIP** *For a quick lunch, make chili in advance and refrigerate. Then just microwave and spoon into insulated container.*

Steve, Age 10

"
My mom calls me 'Souper Man' because I ask her to send soup in my lunch every day. The other kids always want to trade with me, but I won't.
"

## CAESAR CHICKEN SALAD SANDWICHES

**PREP TIME:** 10 MINUTES

1  **can (5 ounces) Swanson® Premium Chunk Chicken Breast, drained**

2  **tablespoons prepared Caesar salad dressing**

1  **tablespoon mayonnaise**

4  **slices Pepperidge Farm® Distinctive Original White *or* Seven Grain Bread**

**Lettuce leaves**

**MIX** chicken, dressing and mayonnaise.

**DIVIDE** chicken mixture between 2 bread slices. Top with lettuce and remaining 2 bread slices.
Makes 2 sandwiches.

"
Sometimes I get notes from my mom. She writes things on the napkin in my lunch, like "I love you." I like those.
"

Christy, Age 10

# Dinner

**Whether a quick meal** in the kitchen after sports practice or a more leisurely meal in the dining room, dinner affords every family the opportunity to experience the joys of gathering around the family table. Conversation and good food, as a daily tradition, brings the generations together.

*Make dinner the one time your family is sure to get together every day*

## EASY PEPPER STEAK

### PREP/COOK TIME: 25 MINUTES

1 pound boneless beef sirloin steak,
   ¾-inch thick*

2 tablespoons vegetable oil

3 cups green *or* red pepper strips

1 medium onion, cut into wedges

½ teaspoon garlic powder

1 can (10¼ ounces) Franco-American® Beef
   Gravy

1 tablespoon Worcestershire sauce

4 cups hot cooked rice

**SLICE** beef into very thin strips.

**HEAT 1 tablespoon** oil in skillet. Add beef and stir-fry until browned and juices evaporate. Push to one side of skillet.

**HEAT** remaining oil. Add peppers, onion and garlic and cook until tender-crisp. Add gravy and Worcestershire. Heat through. Serve over rice. Serves 4.

*To make slicing easier, freeze beef 1 hour.*

**Campbell's**

## BEEF TACO SKILLET

**PREP/COOK TIME:** 20 MINUTES

1 pound ground beef

1 can (10¾ ounces) Campbell's® Tomato Soup

1 cup Pace® Chunky Salsa *or* Picante Sauce

½ cup water

8 flour *or* corn tortillas (6-inch), cut into 1-inch pieces

1 cup shredded Cheddar cheese

**COOK** beef in skillet until browned. Pour off fat.

**ADD** soup, salsa, water, tortillas and **half** the cheese. Heat to a boil. Cover and cook over low heat 5 minutes or until hot.

**TOP** with remaining cheese. Serves 4.

**TIP** *For a smoky flavor next time, add Pace® Chipotle Chunky Salsa instead of Pace® Chunky Salsa.*

## Kitchen Notes

I use a standard box grater to grate cheese. Sometimes, however, as the cheese warms in my hands, it sticks to the grater, both inside and out. My neighbor suggested that I spray the grater lightly with nonstick cooking spray before grating. Now the cheese falls off the grater into the bowl and doesn't stick. The grater is also easier to clean. —*Jenny*

*Campbell's*

## POLYNESIAN PORK CHOPS

**PREP/COOK TIME:** 20 MINUTES

4 boneless pork chops,
  ¾-inch thick

1 teaspoon garlic powder

1 tablespoon vegetable oil

1 medium onion, chopped

1 can (10¾ ounces)
  Campbell's® Golden
  Mushroom Soup

1 can (8 ounces) pineapple
  chunks

¼ cup water

3 tablespoons soy sauce

1 tablespoon honey

2 cups cooked instant
  white rice

Sliced green onions

**SEASON** chops with garlic.

**HEAT** oil in skillet. Add chops and cook until browned. Add onion.

**ADD** soup, pineapple with juice, water, soy and honey. Heat to a boil. Cook over low heat 10 minutes or until done.

**SERVE** with rice and garnish with green onions. Serves 4.

**TIP** *For a quick chicken skillet, use 4 boneless chicken breasts instead of pork chops.*

Kitchen Notes

Once a week, my neighbor celebrates "Travel Night" with her family. She serves a different ethnic or regional cuisine each time, adding fun table décor and music. She even tries to serve an authentic dessert. The whole family loves it! —*Cathy*

## SHRIMP & CORN CHOWDER WITH SUN-DRIED TOMATOES

**PREP/COOK TIME:** 20 MINUTES

1   **can (10¾ ounces) Campbell's® Cream of Potato Soup**

1½  **cups half & half**

2   **cups whole kernel corn**

2   **sun-dried tomatoes packed in oil, drained and cut in strips**

1   **cup small or medium cooked shrimp**

2   **tablespoons chopped fresh chives**

    **Black *or* cayenne pepper**

MIX soup, half & half, corn and tomatoes in saucepan. Heat to a boil.

COOK over low heat 10 minutes. Stir in shrimp and chives and heat through. Season with pepper. Serves 4.

TIP *For a lighter version, use skim milk instead of half & half.*

## Kitchen Notes

I used to watch my mother neatly cut corn off the cob. She would place an ear standing on its end in the tube of an angel food cake pan. Then she would cut straight down the ear with a small paring knife, sending the kernels directly into the pan. —*Cindy*

**Campbell's**®

## GOLDEN CHICKEN WITH NOODLES

| **PREP TIME:** 5 MINUTES | **COOK TIME:** 7 TO 8 HOURS |
| --- | --- |

2　cans (10¾ ounces *each*) Campbell's® Cream of Chicken *or* 98% Fat Free Cream of Chicken Soup

½　cup water

¼　cup lemon juice

1　tablespoon Dijon mustard

1½　teaspoons garlic powder

8　large carrots, thickly sliced

8　boneless chicken breast halves

8　cups hot cooked egg noodles

　Chopped fresh parsley

**MIX** soup, water, lemon juice, mustard, garlic and carrots in slow cooker. Add chicken and turn to coat.

**COVER** and cook on LOW 7 to 8 hours or until done.

**SERVE** over noodles. Sprinkle with parsley. Serves 8.

Kitchen Notes

Your mother probably told you "a watched pot never boils," but she may not have warned you that opening the lid and checking on food in the slow cooker can affect both cooking time and results. Every time you lift the lid, you lose steam. It can take 15 to 20 minutes for your slow cooker to regain lost temperature. Don't peek! —*Jane*

## ROAST CHICKEN WITH STUFFING & GRAVY

**PREP TIME:** 30 MINUTES     **COOK TIME:** 2½ TO 3 HOURS
**STAND TIME:** 10 MINUTES

¼ cup butter *or* margarine

1 stalk celery, sliced

1 medium onion, chopped

1¼ cups water

1 medium carrot, shredded (optional)

4 cups Pepperidge Farm® Herb Seasoned Stuffing

5- to 7-pound roasting chicken

Vegetable oil

1 jar (12 ounces) Franco-American® Slow Roast Chicken Gravy

**HEAT** butter in saucepot. Add celery and onion and cook until tender. Stir in water and carrot. Add stuffing. Mix lightly.

**SPOON** stuffing into neck and body cavities.* Place chicken, breast side up, on rack in shallow roasting pan. Brush with oil.

**ROAST** at 325°F for 2½ to 3 hours or until done, basting occasionally with pan drippings. Allow chicken to stand 10 minutes before slicing. Heat gravy and serve. Serves 6 to 8.

*Bake any remaining stuffing in covered casserole with chicken 30 minutes or until hot.*

## BROCCOLI CHICKEN POTATO PARMESAN

**PREP/COOK TIME:** 20 MINUTES

- 2 **tablespoons vegetable oil**
- 1 **pound small red potatoes, sliced ¼-inch thick**
- 1 **package (about 10 ounces) refrigerated cooked chicken breast strips**
- 2 **cups fresh *or* frozen broccoli flowerets**
- 1 **can (10¾ ounces) Campbell's® Broccoli Cheese *or* 98% Fat Free Broccoli Cheese Soup**
- ½ **cup milk**
- ¼ **teaspoon garlic powder**
- ¼ **cup grated Parmesan cheese**

**HEAT** oil in skillet. Add potatoes. Cover and cook over medium heat 10 minutes, stirring occasionally.

**STIR** in chicken and broccoli.

**MIX** soup, milk and garlic. Add to skillet. Sprinkle with cheese. Heat to a boil. Cover and cook over low heat 5 minutes or until done. Serves 4.

## Kitchen Notes

My Aunt Martha called round red potatoes "boiling potatoes" because she said they had more moisture than most baking potatoes. She swore they made the very best mashed potatoes. —*Jenny*

*Campbell's*®

## TOMATO ROASTED GARLIC STEAK

**PREP/COOK TIME:** 20 MINUTES

1 **can (10¾ ounces) Campbell's® Tomato with Roasted Garlic & Herbs Soup**

½ **cup Italian salad dressing**

1 ½ **pound boneless beef sirloin steak, ¾-inch thick**

**MIX** soup and dressing.

**GRILL** or broil steak to desired doneness (allow 15 minutes for medium), turning once and brushing often with sauce.

**HEAT** remaining sauce to a boil and serve with steak. Serves 6.

**TIP** *For another barbecue favorite, brush sauce on chicken vegetable kabobs.*